Living Words

A Booklet for Renewal in the Holy Spirit

D1350730

MICHAEL HURLEY

Published by Messenger Publications, 2020
Copyright © Michael Hurley, 2020

ISBN 9781788122962

Designed by Messenger Publications Design Department
Cover Image: Solomnikov / Shutterstock
Typeset in Adobe Caslon Pro & Bernhard Modern
Printed by GPS Colour Graphics Ltd

Messenger Publications,
37 Leeson Place, Dublin D02 E5V0
www.messenger.ie

CONTENTS

Section 1

An Introduction to Living Words

Chapter 1: God's Plan for Your Life

'ONLY when we meet the living God in Christ do we know what life is. We are not some casual and meaningless product of evolution. Each of us is the result of a thought of God. Each of us is willed; each of us is loved; each of us is necessary. There is nothing more beautiful than to be surprised by the Gospel, by the encounter with Christ. There is nothing more beautiful than to know Him and to speak to others of our friendship with Him.'[1]

No matter who you are, no matter how you see yourself, no matter what your past, Jesus Christ wants to reveal his personal love for you and fill your heart. He wishes to transform you. He wants to take you on a personal journey when, gradually, and at times suddenly, you will know a deeper trust in his love and live with greater joy, enthusiasm, conviction and love. My hope for you is that he will use the daily reflections in this booklet as a support and encouragement along this journey.

God has a plan for your life. He is not directing or speaking to you from a distance. Rather, he wishes to draw near to you and be intimately involved in your life. He invites you to walk with him along his unique path for

1   Pope Benedict XVI, St Peter's Square, Rome, 24 April 2005.

you. However, God is often perceived as one who, from a distance, sets fixed standards to which people are to measure up, while unconcerned about the burdens and traumas they carry. He thus continues to intrigue them. They may read, study, think and even pray, yet they fail to grasp his unique plan and love for them. God remains at a distance for them and, in a sense, keeps them guessing about who he is and how they are to relate to him.

However, the images of God and of his plan that emerge from the scriptures reveal him as near and involved. God, speaking through the prophet Jeremiah, for example, says very simply and clearly, 'I know the plans I have for you … plans for your welfare and not for harm, to give you a future with hope' (Jer 29:11). In the context, I understand this to mean that God is involved and interested in every event of which I am part. He is present, and his influence points me on the way of peace, even as I live through a disastrous or crushing trauma. He is at work at the core of life's varied and ever-changing circumstances. He announces peace and makes peace possible, within oneself and in one's relationships and undertakings. He inspires us 'to do justice, and to love kindness, and to walk humbly with your God' (Mic 6:8).

In Jesus, God draws close. He establishes peace at the core of existence and in the heart of every person. In his time, Jesus identified with people, and especially in their weakness, failure and sin. He loved each person in a total way to the point of yielding up his life. Now risen, he assures us that no one 'has greater love than this, to lay down one's life for one's friends' (Jn 15:13). He loves totally, to the point of yielding all.

In this way, too, he brings about and establishes reconciliation at the heart of all that exists so that all people share a communion with God and with one another. He now continues to love in this total way. He is ever at work seeking to welcome, to embrace and to forgive every person, whatever their need and misery (Lk 15:1–32). He lives among us. He continues his work of reconciling and peace-bearing among us. Indeed, he lives in each of us. We carry him as in a temple. We are temples of his presence.

Divine loving is not something abstract. It is not an intellectual ideal. It is not limited to a human longing for peace and harmony. Rather, divine loving in the risen Christ is love poured out that reaches towards every aspect of our existence and is carried within our most insignificant thought and event. There is a beautiful passage in Matthew's Gospel, which tells us of God's concern for every facet of human existence. He desires to give us food to eat and clothes to wear and to heal our anxieties and fears (Mt 6:25–34). Even the greatest disasters do not draw a veil over the love that God has for us: 'Who will separate us from the love of Christ? Will hardship, or distress, or persecution, or famine, or nakedness, or peril, or sword?' (Rom 8:35).

The Good News Awaits You

This is not to be interpreted as solely a private, inward-focused journey. Rather, God calls you beyond your own self to make a difference in your family, community and world. He reveals for you a pathway of loving. He proclaimed and lived unconditional love for all, even his enemies.[2] In

2 'Love your enemies, do good to those who hate you' (Lk 6:27; cf, Lk 6:28–29, 35; Mt 5:43–48).

him, divine loving, in and for each individual, opens out as respect and love for all people. In particular, it embraces and commits to one's enemies. This, for Tertullian, remains the distinctive feature of Christianity. He saw that 'all people love their friends, but only Christians love their enemies'.[3]

Jesus Christ, the risen Lord, also calls you to witness to his presence and influence in your life. This involves a deliberate decision on your part, since sharing of personal faith in God runs counter to a prevailing aspect of our culture. Faith today is often 'silenced' in and excluded from the public spheres of Irish life.[4] Perhaps even more unbelievably, such 'silence' is also a reality among people of the Church, as they sadly keep expressions of their personal faith to themselves.

I have read some findings of surveys and commentators to determine the extent to which individual Catholics attempt to share their faith with other people. Findings agree that only a very small percentage has an outward evangelistic reaching attitude. Alvin Illig, for example, estimates that less than 2 per cent of a typical Catholic congregation have an evangelising attitude.[5] In other words, 98 per cent relate to the Church as to a spiritual filling station, where they commune in a private way with God. Faith, then, becomes a pious activity. It seeks personal peace through taking part in rituals and in reciting prayers. At its extreme, this can be

3   Tertullian, *Ad Scapulam*, 1.3.
4   Dermot Ahern, as minister for justice, verbalised this trend, when on local radio he outlined the framework of his thinking in relation to political legislaton. 'When I legislate, particularly as a government minister, I don't bring whatever religion I have to the table' (*The Irish Catholic*, 30 July 2009, 13). He gave this explanation when giving details about the Civil Partnership Bill, which would give to same sex couples almost all of the same rights and benefits as married heterosexual couples.
5   Fr Alvin Illig is the Director of the Paulist National Evangelization Association in the US.

the constant quest for new 'religious' experiences, or reliance on a great comforter to escape the pain of living, while not addressing issues. We end up with 'over-eating' and 'over-weight' Catholics, whose continuing demand is for new experiences, extra Masses, more novenas and, possibly, private revelations. Sharing faith has ceased to be a priority. Rather, we stay in the safety of a 'private' faith and lament that so many of our children and adults do not relate to the Church.

The voice of God, however, can never be silenced. David Barrett, for example, claims, 'The world is more religious than ever; almost every kind of religion has come back as a decisive factor in human life.'[6] We can see the truth of this through a visit to any religious bookshop, with its vast array of tapes, videos, books and magazines. A new interest in Eastern religions exists. There is the rapid growth of new religious movements. There is the explosion in non-Christian literature, which promises meaning and fulfilment. There is the human potential movement with its claims that we can heal ourselves, and that we carry within us the destiny of our own lives without any reference to a personal God. Where the Christian Church is not making the richness of its life available, it runs the risk of being left on the sidelines. When there are too few Christian mentors, people will not look towards the Christian faith to meet their need for belonging, meaning and healing. The evidence is that they look elsewhere to fill an emotional and spiritual vacuum.

We cannot silence the voice of transcendence. God, however we now understand him, simply has a way of

6   David A. Barrett, *World Christian Encyclopedia*, Oxford: Oxford University Press, 1982.

speaking to the heart. The context of this little booklet is precisely an awareness of the living influence of Jesus in the lives of people who have been transformed in his Spirit. This context is also supported, and foretold, by the life and promises of Jesus. He told us, for example, why he came. 'I came that they may have life, and have it abundantly' (Jn 10:10). He also promised us access to the Father's love. 'Ask and it will be given to you; search and you will find' (Mt 7:7).

The daily reflections in *Living Words* are intended to help you to relate with Jesus who wishes to fill your heart, and lead you to live with joy and freedom. You may have many difficulties with faith, Church and even God. Sexual abuse of children by clergy and religious, for example, may have totally broken your trust. You may have considered that your Christian beliefs were part of the right creed or religion but led by the wrong people. Moreover, you may never have felt that you were mentored in the Christian faith. Indeed, there may have been many reasons your relationship with Christ remained at a great distance.

May you find encouragement in the experiences of many prophets. Jeremiah, for example, wished to turn away from God when his faith was challenged, and when he felt treated as a laughing stock. He claims, 'If I say, "I will not mention him or speak any more in his name," then within me there is something like a burning fire shut up in my bones; I am weary with holding it in, and I cannot' (Jer 20:9). May you too experience the 'burning fire' of God deep within you. May you know that you are caught up in a mystery of loving that is too big for you to understand. May you grow in fascination of Jesus and of his plan for you.

The problem for us as Christians is not that we expect too much but that we expect too little from God. We fear that if we expect a lot we will be disappointed. The truth is that his voice and influence can never be silenced. He is at work to draw us from mediocrity towards mystery, presence and freedom. He leads us from what is too often 'normal Christianity', when we settle for a faith that is scarcely Christian in being limited, overly rational and confined within the horizons and limits of self. He is ever at work leading us to Christianity, which is ever beyond our grasp and is relational, open-ended and rooted in the freedom to love and serve. In responding to his leading we too find our unique dignity as children of God.

This is God's gift to us. It is his call to us. It is his vision for our lives. It is about his finding us beyond our search. It is more about being surprised and grasped by God's Spirit than the result of our seeking and searching. At the same time it is over to us. It is about yielding, and opening hands and hearts in awe and welcome. In the words of St Augustine, 'He who created you without your consent will not save you without your cooperation.'[7]

Pope Francis echoes somewhat similar thinking. He understands that 'there is the resurrection of the body, which takes place on the last day. But, remember there is also the resurrection of the heart, which can happen daily.' For him, then, the Risen one is now always present transforming hearts to arise to new life, sing his praises, and live in service of the new world he makes possible.

7   St Augustine, Sermon 169, 13 (PL 38,923).

Chapter 2: Renewed in the Holy Spirit

A MYSTERIOUS influence is at work within you. It is the presence of the Holy Spirit. He invites you to a transformation of thinking and of lifestyle: 'to be renewed in the spirit of your minds, and to clothe yourselves with the new self, created according to the likeness of God in true righteousness and holiness' (Eph 4:23–24). Here he invites you to recognise your deeper, richer and more real self, so that it surrounds and shelters you as does a garment. You obviously have a part to play. However, it is not primarily your doing. It first of all has its roots in the action of the Holy Spirit. It then becomes your response to God's grace.

Paul, writing to Titus, announces that transformation happens because God 'saved us, not because of any works of righteousness that we had done, but according to his mercy, through the water of rebirth and renewal by the Holy Spirit' (Titus 3:5). For Paul, the Holy Spirit is at the source of all that happens as we journey and struggle, in our relationship with God. Without him, we will never recognise that 'Jesus is Lord' (1 Cor 12:3). This is your journey now too. It moves you away from a preoccupation with your strengths and weaknesses, achievements and failures, to seeing what God's Holy Spirit wishes to do in your life.

The death of Jesus had a terrible effect on his followers. They had such great hopes when they followed him. They looked forward to freedom from the Roman authorities.

They would have places of influence with him. Now all lay in ruins. All was dashed. The one they followed had been put to death. Their dream was over. They looked upon what they had done as a bad phase of life. How could they have been so naive? So gullible? It was now time to return to the work they had left behind, their fishing places, their small farms and businesses.

But it was not even that simple for them. They knew they lived in real danger. They, like their leader, could be put to death. So they huddled together to make sense of what had happened and to feel somewhat secure.

Strange reports began to spread that Jesus had risen, and that he had appeared to some women, to Peter, to the two men who were going back to Emmaus from Jerusalem. However, nothing could have prepared them for the event on that first Pentecost. Luke records it in Acts of the Apostles. 'All of them were filled with the Holy Spirit and began to speak in other languages, as the Spirit gave them the ability' (Acts 2:4).

The people of Jerusalem who saw this happen were 'amazed and astonished' and could not explain it. The only thing they could think of was that these people must be drunk. Peter began to explain what had really happened. He spoke about Jesus becoming man, how he lived, that he was put to death and that 'this Jesus God raised up, and of that all of us are witnesses' (Acts 2:32). He concluded, 'he has poured out this that you both see and hear' (Acts 2:33). It was remarkable how a frightened, timid, almost broken group of people could undergo such a transformation.

The impact was immediate. Those listening were, in Luke's words, 'cut to the heart' (Acts 2:37), and asked how what had happened to the disciples could happen for them. Peter explained, 'Repent, and be baptized every one of you in the name of Jesus Christ so that your sins may be forgiven; and you will receive the gift of the Holy Spirit' (Acts 2:38). The result was that on 'that very day about three thousand were added to their number' (Acts 2:41).

Ever since, this has been the paradigm and template for what happens among the followers of Christ. Transformation and renewal begin as individuals come to see, touch and know the Holy Spirit as the Lord and giver of life. The Holy Spirit is the principal agent. He now wishes to transform your life, and as you hear and experience his good news, you will recognise a desire to share it with other people. You, too, will know that a new Pentecost will precede and inspire an evangelisation that is new.

We have seen that, at the first Pentecost, God's Holy Spirit transformed an unlikely band of followers of Jesus and empowered them to speak to the people of their day and lead them to Christ. This was the way Jesus intended it to be. He had promised that he would send the Spirit. He would clothe his followers 'with power from on high' (Lk 24:29). He said they would 'receive power when the Holy Spirit has come upon you; and you will be my witnesses ... to the ends of the earth' (Acts 1:8). He promised that 'when the spirit of truth comes, he will guide you into all the truth' (Jn 16:13).

For God's people transformation and renewal are not

the result of human effort and achievement. We may be tempted to think that they depend on our own planning, preparation, learning and strength. Yes, these may help, but personal renewal is always, at its deepest, a response to the active presence of God's Spirit. He invites us to journey with him to the place of mystery, deep within us, where he resides. Here is the place of stillness from which issues forth peace, wisdom, conviction and commitment. Without him, Christian living remains empty and lifeless, without direction or enthusiasm.

This thinking finds great resonance in the thinking of Pope Francis, who appeals for Spirit-filled followers of Christ. He calls for approaches and activities that are inspired by the Holy Spirit. He calls for a movement of prayer so that people will show great boldness in proclaiming the newness of the Gospel. 'At Pentecost, the Spirit made apostles go forth from themselves and turned them into heralds of God's wondrous deeds, capable of speaking to each person in his or her own language. The Holy Spirit also grants the courage to proclaim the newness of the Gospel with boldness in every time and place, even when it meets with opposition. Let us call upon him today, firmly rooted in prayer, for without prayer all our activity risks being fruitless and our message empty.'[8]

The fact that you continue to read this booklet suggests that the Spirit of God wishes to do a great work in you and open a new chapter for you. He invites you into a new experience of his love and dynamic presence. You can now trust the movement of his mysterious influence as he guides

8   Pope Francis, *Evangelii Gaudium*, 24 November 2013, 259.

you along the path of his unique plan for you. In the words of Pope Francis, 'Don't cage the Spirit of God'. Reach out to God's Spirit. Take hold of and accept the new freedom and life he is offering you.

Come, Holy Spirit, fills the hearts of the faithful and enkindle in them the fire of your love.

Chapter 3: What You Can Expect to Experience

MY HOPE is that as you use *Living Words* you will become more aware that God is your freedom and peace; that he dwells deep within you; and that the mysterious power and influence of his Spirit will surprise you. In this way, you will know a deepening of faith in God, grow in trust of him, and take on greater responsibility for your life before him.

You will learn to speak to God in a more personal way. The time that you set aside each day will become important moments when you commune alone with God. Here you will find a deepening sense of his love for you and of his plan for your life. The important thing here is that you decide on a time and find a reasonably comfortable place where you know you will not be disturbed. What happens at Sunday worship tends to be simply words unless on Monday you relate with God in silence and let him touch the complexities of your life.

Jesus said very little about prayer, except to encourage his followers to pray. One learns to pray by doing it. Remember that there is no one way to pray. You will find your way. As you grow in silence, and as you listen, you will gradually come to know the distinctive prayer of the Holy Spirit within you. He is your helper during times when you know weakness, and may not even know for what you should pray. He then intervenes, prays in you and pleads before God for you, 'with sighs too deep for words' (Rom 8:26). All the time, he leads you to know that in all things he is at work for your good and that nothing can separate you from God's assuring love (Rom 8:28, 38–39).

The scriptures will open up to you as the word of God. In your quiet time, ask God to speak to you through the passage assigned for the particular day. It is his word. Then read it. After some silence, read it again. Allow yourself to be drawn to a phrase or thought. At times it happens that you may think it has said very little, yet later during the day it comes to mind as being especially relevant to a particular situation or event. This is the word of God for you. It is alive and active. You can expect that most of the passages will speak very directly and clearly to you. In this way you will come to a conviction about the scriptures as God's word, and a facility in opening the Bible and using it while you pray.

The gift of faith will become more than ever good news for you. You will also become more confident in engaging in dialogue with others who may have very different perspectives. Comfortable in your own identity, you will no longer see the need to win arguments, but will relate to all on the basis of respect. You will see each person as a child of God. You will likely grow alert to passing on faith in loving and appropriate ways. You may also feel challenged about how you can best contribute to your relationships and the world around you.

You may gain confidence in encouraging a family time of reflection and conversation. You may, for example, begin to use the school religious programme with your child. I know of one parent whose children, all young adults, no longer attend Mass. She admits that she relates to them no longer on the basis that they should attend, but rather at the level of the values that are important to them. This has enabled her to listen to them, share with them about values and offer her own story of the influence of God in her life.

You will learn of the influence of the Holy Spirit. Throughout the New Testament there are listings of gifts of the Holy Spirit. They are not intended to be exhaustive. These gifts are called manifestations and demonstrations of the Spirit. We find them in 1 Corinthians 12:7–11, 28–30; Ephesians 4; Romans 12:7 and 1 Peter 4. They include the message of faith, knowledge, healing, miraculous powers, prophecy, tongues, leadership, hospitality, evangelism, pastoring, administration and teaching. The community received its direction, life and energy through the Holy Spirit who made it distinctive from every other grouping. It was not a democracy. Rather, the Spirit inspired gifts in each person, who then served others and heralded the good news according to God's grace at work in their lives. The community of Christ's followers is thus mystical in that it comprises those who experience the Spirit of the Risen Lord, who are inspired by his gifts, and who offer them in service. The gifts of the Spirit were seen to have three purposes for the early Church: a) to lead to a deeper faith in God; b) to build community, the Body of Christ; and c) to awaken an uninterested world.

The world is already tired of words. It needs the demonstration that Christianity works. It looks for signs of God's presence in lives converted by him, as seen especially in the way believers love one another and in their care and love for the poor. It is the Spirit who gives words to those who seek to declare for him before others. It is he who prompts coincidences, signs and awakenings in the hearts of those who hear. It is he who communicates healings and miracles. It was such in the early Church. It is to be the norm for today too. It is now equally available to you.

How to Use this Booklet
You can undertake this series of reflections on your own. You can equally decide to undertake it with other people. During the six weeks, for example, you might meet in an informal setting with a few friends once each week and share what the scriptures, reflections and times of prayer mean for you. You can share how you sense God's presence and what he may be saying to you. A cup of tea or coffee may greatly aid conversation. If you are part of a particular ministry in your parish or community, for example, you might consider undertaking it as a team. As well as being of benefit to individuals, this will also build a team spirit among participants, and communicate direction and vision as a team.

This booklet also serves as a participants' aid for those who undertake the *Inspiring Faith Communities* programme. The advantage in this is that each week for the six weeks of the programme you will hear a presentation introducing you to the theme of the following week. It also has the advantage that you will hear the comments, responses and questions of other people who are following the booklet at this time.

The value of these small groups is that you learn from one another's insights. It shows you the great variety of responses and ways of seeing the same question. It also has the value of giving you the opportunity of speaking about faith. In this way, you form a close bond with others present. You come to appreciate other viewpoints shared, which may lead you to think differently. It may surprise and greatly inspire you to hear someone you already know speak about the importance of God or prayer in his or her life. You will likely be greatly encouraged when you hear of the faith and struggle of another.

I am delighted that you are thinking about using *Living Words* as a basis for your reflections during the coming six weeks. May this be the beginning of an exciting journey for you.

After completing the series of reflections, you may wish to read the final chapter of this booklet where you will find information of one type of support network, which aims to help participants see how faith leads to better relationships with self, others and God. You may think it worth considering as a way of continuing your experience.

One thing is certain. God is nearer to us than we realise. Our ancestors knew this: 'Is giorra cabhair Dé ná an doras' (God's help is closer than the door). God has more in store for you than you may expect. He is nearer to you than you realise.

Section 2

Daily Reflections and Personal Prayer

PRAYER creates an atmosphere where life is simplified. In prayer, we bring to God, who is love, the joys and hardships that crowd in upon us. Prayer has many moods: sometimes we are presenting our struggles; at other times we are expressing our gratitude to God for his goodness. Prayer is always a conversation in which we take on a trusting, childlike attitude before God in the certainty of his love and providence.

Living Words offers a scripture passage and a brief reflection for each day of six weeks. The important thing is to decide on a precise time each day for your daily prayer and reflection. It is your sacred time with Jesus. If prayer, as conversation and listening in a personal and spontaneous way, is new for you, then you may decide to set aside ten or fifteen minutes each day.

Select a comfortable place where you are unlikely to be disturbed. You may like to start with a few moments to become quiet. It may help you to become aware of the movement of your breath. Then make a short prayer that the Spirit of God will guide you during your time with him. Read the scripture passage through and then, after a period of silence, read it a second time, allowing it to become for you a living word. The reflection given is simply to act as an aid to a deeper trust in God. You may wish to conclude with a prayer of thanksgiving for what you have heard, and to invite God to help you in living out his word during the rest of the day.

For some, *Living Words* is used for personal reflection and prayer during the *Inspiring Faith Communities* programme. In this instance, Week 1, Day 1 is for the day after the first presentation of the programme. The thoughts for each week are linked to the themes of your meetings.

Pope Francis describes prayer as coming with open hearts before the gaze of love. He then goes on to say that 'the best incentive for sharing the Gospel comes from contemplating it with love, lingering over its pages and reading it with the heart. If we approach it in this way, its beauty will amaze and constantly excite us. But if this is to come about, we need to recover a contemplative spirit which can help us to realise ever anew that we are entrusted with a treasure which makes us more human and helps us to lead a new life.'[9]

9   Pope Paul VI, *Evangelii Nuntiandi, on Evangelisation in the Modern World*, 8 December 1975, 264.

Week 1

Day 1

Unbind him, and let him go. (Jn 11:44)

Jesus spoke these words to Lazarus as he restored him to life from his place of death in the tomb. Listen today to the voice and the mind of Christ as he speaks to you in your particular situation. What binds you? Where do you desire to be free?

Day 2

There was no water for the people to drink. The people quarreled with Moses. (Ex 17:1–2)

'Thus you shall say to the house of Jacob, and tell the Israelites: You have seen what I did to the Egyptians, and how I bore you on eagles' wings and brought you to myself. Now therefore, if you obey my voice and keep my covenant, you shall be my treasured possession out of all peoples. Indeed, the whole earth is mine, but you shall be for me a priestly kingdom and a holy nation' … So Moses came, summoned the elders of the people, and set before them all these words that the Lord has commanded him. The people answered as one 'Everything that the Lord has spoken we will do.' (Ex 19:4–8)

The people of Israel lived through times of constant change as they continued their journey out of slavery towards the Promised Land. They forgot about God's guidance of them, and about his faithfulness. They forgot how much he was on their side. Instead they grumbled and complained. They blamed Moses. Amid the complaints, the accusations and the uncertainties of today, you, too, can rely on God's faithfulness. He remains faithful to you. He is calling you to himself. Let his word for you this day speak to your heart.

Day 3

> Therefore I tell you, do not worry about your life, what you will eat or what you will drink, or about your body, what you will wear. Is not life more than food, and the body more than clothing? Look at the birds of the air; they neither sow nor reap nor gather into barns, and yet your heavenly Father feeds them. Are you not of more value than they? And can any of you by worrying add a single hour to your span of life? And why do you worry about clothing? Consider the lilies of the field, how they grow; they neither toil nor spin, yet I tell you, even Solomon in all his glory was not clothed like one of these. But if God so clothes the grass of the field, which is alive today and tomorrow is thrown into the oven, will he not much more clothe you – you of little faith? Therefore do not worry, saying, 'What will we eat?' or 'What will we drink?' or 'What will we wear?' For it is the Gentiles who strive for all these

things; and indeed your heavenly Father knows that you need all these things. But strive first for the kingdom of God and his righteousness, and all these things will be given to you as well. (Mt 6:25–33)

In this scripture passage Jesus speaks to the restless spirit and the anxious heart. He tells us about divine providence, and about God who is eager to provide for us. The scripture brings us face to face with personal worry and how we can best deal with it. It invites us to look at nature and to see its patterns. The birds of the air possess a beauty much greater than the splendour of Solomon. We can plant a seed in the soil and we can water it, but only God gives the growth.

This scripture tells us about God's commitment to our well-being and his concern for the details of life. He knows when a sparrow falls from a rooftop. He feeds the birds and grows the flowers. There is nothing too small that he does not notice and continues to create. He has numbered every hair on our heads, or, indeed for some of us, he sees how many have already fallen away. He knows, too, when we are hungry and naked, and will nourish and clothe us. We can totally trust that he will provide us with whatever we need. Take a few moments as you listen to the scripture passage or to a particular word, phrase or image, and let a sense of God's providential love for you surface.

Day 4

For it is God who is at work in you, enabling you both to will and to work for his good pleasure.

25

Do all things without murmuring and arguing, so that you may be blameless and innocent, children of God without blemish in the midst of a crooked and perverse generation, in which you shine like stars in the world. It is by your holding fast to the word of life that I can boast on the day of Christ that I did not run in vain or labour in vain. (Phil 2:13–16)

God is at work in your life. He is inspiring in you a prayer, a generosity and a wish to serve him. He has promised that you will be a light for him in the world and you will be offering others the opportunity to find new life in him. Thank God who is near you. Thank him for who you are at this time in your life and for the desires he places on your heart.

Day 5

But as for you, continue in what you have learned and firmly believed, knowing from whom you learned it, and how from childhood you have known the sacred writings that are able to instruct you for salvation through faith in Christ Jesus. All scripture is inspired by God and is useful for teaching, for reproof, for correction, and for training in righteousness, so that everyone who belongs to God may be proficient, equipped for every good work. (2 Tim 3:14–17)

'Ignorance of scripture is ignorance of Christ' (St Jerome). The scriptures are God's word for your life. They are God's gift to you so that you can come to know him and also be equipped to work effectively with him. So let his words seep into the deepest parts of your life.

Today thank God for your 'teachers'. Recall, with gratitude, those who have influenced you, those who have been your role models through the example of their lives, through their words and, above all, through the love you knew they had for you.

Day 6

Abide in me as I abide in you. Just as the branch cannot bear fruit by itself unless it abides in the vine, neither can you unless you abide in me. I am the vine, you are the branches. Those who abide in me and I in them bear much fruit, because apart from me you can do nothing. (Jn 15:4–5)

I appointed you to go and bear fruit, fruit that will last (Jn 15:16)

Jesus calls you to make a difference and to bear fruit. He invites you to a deeper trust in him and to remain close to him. Let his gaze of love rest upon you today. Abide and rest in his love. He will lead you to look outwards in love towards all. Your faith is not to remain dormant and passive but is to lead to action and service that benefits other people and the world in which you live. Then your faith will impact the culture and the relationships within which you operate.

Day 7

For the mountains may depart
and the hills be removed,
but my steadfast love shall not depart from you,
and my covenant of peace shall not be removed,
says the Lord, who has compassion on you. (Isa 54:10)

Ho, everyone who thirsts,
come to the waters;
and you that have no money,
come, buy and eat!
come, buy wine and milk
without money and without price. (Isa 55:1)

You may think that your resources are scarce – that you have little to give. You may think that you have few answers for the issues and difficulties of life. You may think that you are helpless in the face of much that happens around you and to you. You may even feel empty and dry, with little zest for life. Well, listen again to God's word for you. He is speaking personally to you. He is making promises to you.

Week 2

Day 1

> Now when Jesus came into the district of
> Caesarea Philippi, he asked his disciples, 'Who
> do people say that the Son of Man is?' And they
> said, 'Some say John the Baptist, but others Elijah,
> and still others Jeremiah or one of the prophets.'
> (Mt 16:13–14)

No doubt, you too have heard what people today say about
Jesus. Now it is your turn to answer. Jesus, risen and alive
today, turns to you. He is not seeking a profound answer
from you. On your part, gently relax, rest and be comfortable.
In your own time, recognise the sense of who Jesus is that
arises to your awareness. Take a few moments while it grows
clearer for you. Jesus now invites you to speak. Tell him your
answer. Imagine what you might say to him. Imagine what
he might say to you.

Day 2

> Then Jesus, filled with the power of the Spirit,
> returned to Galilee, and a report about him
> spread through all the surrounding country.
> (Lk 4:14)

> When he came to Nazareth, where he had been
> brought up, he went to the synagogue on the

sabbath day, as was his custom. He stood up to read, and the scroll of the prophet Isaiah was given to him. He unrolled the scroll and found the place where it was written:

'The Spirit of the Lord is upon me,
because he has anointed me
to bring good news to the poor.
He has sent me to proclaim release to the captives
and recovery of sight to the blind,
to let the oppressed go free,
to proclaim the year of the Lord's favor.'
(Lk 4:16–19)

Jesus tells us why he came. He gives us his mission statement. The Spirit of God has anointed him for a purpose. He comes to bring good news.

He now pays you a personal visit. Thank him for coming. Listen to what he is saying to you in this passage. Imagine yourself quietly sitting with him. You are listening. How does this make you feel? What is he saying to you? What is your response?

Conclude your time with some words of thanksgiving of your own. You can use 'Questions on Luke 4' (page 34), if it is of benefit to you.

Day 3

Being therefore exalted at the right hand of God, and having received from the Father the promise of the Holy Spirit, he has poured out this that you both see and hear. (Acts 2:33)

30

DUPS.

11/12/20.

13.05.15

13.05.15

13.05.15
13.05.15

13.05.15
13.05.15

13.05.15

God had a great plan. He wished to rescue his people and make possible a new way of living for them. He sent Jesus into the world to reveal his love. Jesus lived in union with the Father and loved all whom he met. His love was so total that he gave all to the point of death. People were touched by his love, which they saw in visible and physical ways. Jesus also promised to send the Holy Spirit. Then, when the Father embraced him and raised him up, the Holy Spirit was released in the world to continue the work of Jesus in new and powerful ways.

Be filled with wonder at the mystery of God's plan. Love alone inspires it. You may be able to identify ways that reveal the influence of the Holy Spirit at work today. Allow a sense of gratitude to arise within you.

Remember, too, that the Holy Spirit has so much more to give you. 'The Advocate, the Holy Spirit, whom the Father will send in my name, will teach you everything and remind you of all I have said to you' (Jn 14:26).

Day 4

> When Jesus heard this, he said to them, 'Those who are well have no need of a physician, but those who are sick; I have come to call not the righteous but sinners.' (Mk 2:17)

Let this inspire you to draw closer to Jesus. You can be honest with him and speak to him. He is not seeking a perfect caste around him. Rather, sinners act as magnets for his love. They attract him. Our sin, failings and poverty can teach us about his love and mercy for us. Speak to him about them.

The English mystic, Julian of Norwich, declared in 1375, 'Sin is necessary, but all shall be well, and all shall be well, and all manner of things shall be well.'

Day 5

> Jesus said to him, 'I am the way, and the truth, and the life. No one comes to the Father except through me. (Jn 14:6)

Jesus here makes some extraordinary claims. He outlines the way that we as Christians are to travel. And when we walk in his footsteps, we come to know truth and live the deepest reality of life with purpose and meaning.

This way, truth and life are not objective standards for you to achieve. Neither are they impersonal. 'I am' suggests a rich meaning. Yes, Jesus embodies them. He is the Way. He is the Truth. He is the Life.

Jesus looks directly towards you. He is all you need to live with gratitude and authenticity. Now be present before him and let your heart respond to him.

Day 6

> Abide in me as I abide in you (Jn 15:4)

Sit still, become comfortable. Close your eyes gently. Home is a place. Imagine your favourite home. Home is equally a feeling and state of contentment. You may use the phrase 'being at home with myself' to describe the feeling when you know you are totally accepted, happy to be who you are and, indeed, seen as you are. Feel this sense of acceptance. Hear

Jesus as he invites you to a relationship of deep intimacy. You are in him. Now rest in him. Find your home in him. Equally, he is in you. He dwells within you. He loves in you. He prays in you.

Sit with him in the home of his love. Know that he is at prayer in you. Hear his prayer. Let it take you to a place of deep silence.

Day 7

Although he was a Son, he learned obedience
through what he suffered; and having been made
perfect, he became the source of eternal salvation
for all who obey him (Heb 5:9)

An incredible thought. Jesus learns the meaning of love through suffering. Love for the Father and for you leads to his ignominious death. It seems like a failure. But this is not the end. Love triumphs. Here is a beginning. Jesus now is 'the source of eternal salvation' for you. So hear him inviting you to walk with him. 'Come, follow me' (Mt 9:9), he whispers to you. He asks, can you now walk the way of loving? Can you announce, and be, good news for the poor (in your own poverty and wherever you meet it). He promises that in this way you will find salvation in him and that he will raise you up.

Simply be present to this great mystery. Thank Jesus for his deep love for you. Thank him for his plan for you. Listen to the feelings this evokes for you. End this time of reflection with a brief prayer in your own words.

Questions on Luke 4

Some of the following questions may, or may not, help you to listen to God's word.

A)

- What is your poverty? Self-image? Finances? Love? Companionship? Difficulty in receiving? Difficulty in giving?
- Where might you be captive? Pain? Addiction? Depression? Fear? A pattern of sin? Negative thinking about yourself or another? Feelings of being trapped?
- What does being blind mean for you? Little insight about who you are? Failure to see the goodness in another? Keeping God at a distance?
- Where are you downtrodden? Crushed by some past event? Dominated by another?

B)

- How can you be good news to someone you know who appears to be poor?
- How can you announce freedom for those who are captive?
- How can you bring sight to the blind?
- Who are the downtrodden around you?

Stay with any question(s) that provoke strong feelings. To end your time of reflection simply thank Jesus for his presence and invite his continued healing.

Week 3

Day 1

> Philip found Nathanael and said to him, 'We have found him about whom Moses in the law and also the prophets wrote, Jesus son of Joseph from Nazareth.' Nathanael said to him, 'Can anything good come out of Nazareth?' Philip said to him, 'Come and see.' (Jn 1:45–46)

One friend invites another. The discovery of good news is followed with inviting family and friends to share in it. When you wish to pass on faith to others, what are you inviting them to come and see? Is it to come and see the relationship of friendship that Jesus desires to have with them? Is it to come and see where Christianity is lived and where people find support to live with deep faith? In your prayer today ask for the grace that you can take the place of Philip as you relate to your family and friends. Listen to the promptings of Christ in your life and hear his vision for your life.

Day 2

> And Jesus came and said to them, 'All authority in heaven and on earth has been given to me. Go therefore and make disciples of all nations, baptising them in the name of the Father and of the Son and of the Holy Spirit, and teaching them to obey everything that I have commanded

you. And remember, I am with you always, to the
end of the age. (Mt 28:18–20)

Jesus is commanding his disciples to look outwards. He is
sending them with his authority to be active and to make
disciples. To whom are you being sent with the authority
of Christ? Who are the people in your world? You are
meeting them each day as you go about your daily work.
You evangelise as you go; you don't need to go to evangelise.
In your prayer today bring before the Lord those whom you
meet each day, pray for the gift of love for each of them and
for the gift of courage to be able to speak words of faith
sensitively at opportune times.

Day 3

But you will receive power when the Holy Spirit
has come upon you; and you will be my witnesses
in Jerusalem, in all Judea and Samaria, and to the
ends of the earth. (Acts 1:8)

There can be no evangelisation without the cooperation of the Holy Spirit – he suggests to
every preacher of the gospel the right words
which he alone could provide and at the same
time predisposes the minds of the hearers to a
full acceptance of the gospel … we urge all the
heralds of the gospel, whatever be their order
or rank, to pray unceasingly to the divine Spirit
with faith and ardour and to submit themselves
prudently to his guidance as the principal
author of their plans, of their initiatives and

their work in the field of evangelisation.[10]

The Lord wishes to empower you with a new gift of the Holy Spirit so you can reach others in his name.

Day 4

> So they called them and ordered them not to speak or teach at all in the name of Jesus. But Peter and John answered them, 'Whether it is right in God's sight to listen to you rather than to God, you must judge; for we cannot keep from speaking about what we have seen and heard.' (Acts 4:18–20)

The present world may not seem receptive in giving a place to the message of Christ. Can you dare to ask God for the conviction, confidence and courage that you see in Peter and John?

Day 5

> If I proclaim the gospel, this gives me no ground for boasting, for an obligation is laid on me, and woe to me if I do not proclaim the gospel! (1 Cor 9:16)

Baptism and confirmation make us part of God's people and empower us to be witnesses. It is a privilege to be an evangelist. It is to be graced and gifted by God for mission. Paul seeks every opportunity to announce the good news of Jesus Christ. He gives thanks to God by living out the

10 *Evangelii Nuntiandi*, 75.

privilege that was his as evangelist and witness. Without such witness God's grace lies dormant.

Day 6

> But how are they to call on one in whom they have not believed? And how are they to believe in one of whom they have never heard? And how are they to hear without someone to proclaim him? And how are they to proclaim him unless they are sent? (Rom 10:14–15)

The only gospel that some people will read or see may be what they observe in the example of your life and hear from the words of your lips. Your witness will encourage others to call upon the name of the Lord. To whom are you sent?

Day 7

> So they remained for a long time, speaking boldly for the Lord, who testified to the word of his grace by granting signs and wonders to be done through them. (Acts 14:3)

It is always a risk to share your faith. It (and you) may not be understood. You may feel that you know very little and may fear being 'found out', if the other responds and asks for a deeper understanding of faith. But your confidence is not in what *you* know but in God. He promises that when you take risks for him, you will be supported. You will be given his wisdom in difficult situations: 'for I will give you words and a wisdom that none of your opponents will be able to withstand or contradict' (Lk 21:15).

Week 4

This week you will write your good news story, your story of faith. Decide now on a time that you will set aside to write it. See page 56 for guidelines.

Day 1

> We have seen the Lord. (Jn 20:25)

In the scriptures there are many examples of the Lord meeting people in a way that takes account of their personal histories. To the disciples, who were filled with fear, he offered peace: 'Peace be with you'; to Thomas, who needed physical touch and proof, he showed his hands and his side; to the two disciples who knew the Old Testament, he explained the prophecies in the scriptures about Jesus; he called Mary, who was alone and lonely, by name; he stopped Paul, a strong and independent personality, in his tracks on the road so that his companions had to take him by the hand. Invite God's Spirit to guide you to see his personal love and guidance in your story. Thank him for the time(s) you can say, 'I have seen the Lord.'

Day 2

> Paul, an apostle of Christ Jesus by the command
> of God our Savior and of Christ Jesus our hope,
> To Timothy, my loyal child in the faith:
> Grace, mercy, and peace from God the Father
> and Christ Jesus our Lord. (1 Tim 1:1–2)

Paul had great affection for Timothy. God sends people into our lives. Take time to recall the significant people in your life who have influenced you to be a person of faith. In them you can see God's goodness to you. Thank God for each of them. They are very likely central figures in your faith story.

Day 3

> Many Samaritans from that city believed in him because of the woman's testimony, 'He told me everything I have ever done.' So when the Samaritans came to him, they asked him to stay with them; and he stayed there two days. (Jn 4:39–40)

The influence of the testimony of the Samaritan woman is evident. Once she had experienced living water in meeting Jesus, and knew of his acceptance and love for her, she told the people of the town who listened to her story of conviction and truth. They then knew that they too could come to Jesus and 'beg' him to stay with them and to give them living waters. The woman's story had stirred up a curiosity in them to seek and to find Jesus.

Day 4

> Then their eyes were opened, and they recognised him; and he vanished from their sight. They said to each other, 'Were not our hearts burning within us while he was talking to us on the road, while he was opening the scriptures to us?' That

same hour they got up and returned to Jerusalem; and they found the eleven and their companions gathered together. They were saying, 'The Lord has risen indeed, and he has appeared to Simon!' Then they told what had happened on the road, and how he had been made known to them in the breaking of the bread. (Lk 24:31–35)

'That same hour they got up'. One can almost pick up their enthusiasm and excitement. They wanted to tell their story. Who may you tell your story to today? How may your story help another to live life with greater trust and love of the Lord? In your time of prayer, bring these questions to him. Pray daily for an opportunity to share your story for his glory.

Day 5

Blessed be the God and Father of our Lord Jesus Christ, the Father of mercies and the God of all consolation, who consoles us in all our affliction, so that we may be able to console those who are in any affliction with the consolation with which we ourselves are consoled by God. (2 Cor 1:3–4)

There are many elements in one's good news story. One of them is realising the comforting love and providence of God during a time of trial. Let your prayer rise in praise and gratitude to God for his faithfulness even when you have been unfaithful to him, for his mercy when you have wandered from him, and for his comfort and healing at times of great trauma. Ask the Lord to lead you gently to specific reasons for praise and gratitude.

Day 6

> When we had all fallen to the ground, I heard a voice saying to me in the Hebrew language, 'Saul, Saul, why are you persecuting me? It hurts you to kick against the goads.' (Acts 26:14)

> Paul declared in explanation of his conversion event: 'After that, King Agrippa, I was not disobedient to the heavenly vision' (Acts 26:19).

The desire to share one's testimony is a gift. It is like an influence and impulse from within, which seeks opportunities to make the good news available to others. It is not a burden, even when it means risks, misunderstandings and difficulties. It is part of who one is; it is an attitude towards others that they may experience the love of God and the support of his people.

Day 7

> For this reason I remind you to rekindle the gift of God that is within you through the laying on of my hands; for God did not give us a spirit of cowardice, but rather a spirit of power and of love and of self-discipline. Do not be ashamed, then, of the testimony about our Lord or of me his prisoner, but join with me in suffering

for the gospel, relying on the power of God
(2 Tim 1:6–8)

During your time of quiet prayer, allow the Lord to fan into
a flame the influence of his Spirit that is within you. Then
you will have greater confidence and power in witnessing
and in living a Christian life.

Week 5

Day 1

> As he walked along, he saw a man blind from
> birth. (Jn 9:1)

Thank God for who you are. You are a child of God. He
knows you deeply and accepts you as you are, with all your
imperfections and failings. Thank him for the gift of his
Son, Jesus, who heals you of the wounds, blindness and
sinfulness that are part of your life. Thank him for the gift of
his Spirit, who is making all things new, and is offering you
new beginnings. Expect God to inspire gratitude and praise
today during your time of prayer.

Day 2

> I came that they may have life, and have it
> abundantly. (Jn 10:10)

Be present to God as you are. Let God be present to you
face to face. Accept his healing and forgiving love upon you
as a person, or upon a particular area that is surfacing as a
source of worry for you at this time. Hear him calling you
forth to a fullness of life.

Day 3

> Being therefore exalted at the right hand of God,
> and having received from the Father the promise
> of the Holy Spirit, he has poured out this that
> you both see and hear. (Acts 2:33)

As part of your reflection today slowly say the following prayer as you hand your life over to Jesus and invite him to be the one who guides and controls your life:

Lord Jesus Christ, I thank you for all you have done for me. I thank you for suffering death because of the depth of your love for me. I rejoice that you are raised up in glory at the right hand of the Father.

I thank you for the gift of your Spirit. He was not for the early Church alone, but is for me now as I open my hands and my heart to you in prayer. Send forth the outpouring of your Spirit that I may know a conversion of my heart, a forgiveness of my sin, a desire to give my life to you and a confidence in knowing you as Lord of my life. Let there be a new Pentecost now in my life.

I know you always want me to expect great things from you and to bear fruit for your glory. Let all I say and do be ever directed by your promptings. Lead me to rediscover my roots in you and among your people, the Church.

Into your hands I commend my spirit. I trust in your love and providence for me. I bless and thank you for hearing my prayer, which I make in Christ the Lord. Amen.

Day 4

For thus says the Lord God: I myself will search for my sheep, and will seek them out … I will feed them with good pasturage … I myself will be the shepherd of my sheep, and I will make them lie down, says the Lord God. I will seek the lost, and I will bring back the strayed, and I will bind up the injured, and I will strengthen the weak (Ezek 34:11, 14, 15–16)

What extraordinary promises! Be present today to the Lord who speaks these promises to you. He wants to pasture and nourish you. He wants to gather a people who will know his care and love for them. Now listen to his call as you place your total trust in him and in his promises. Imagine and hear him being your shepherd. Hear him teach you what it means to shepherd those whom you meet.

Day 5

> I do not accept glory from human beings … How can you believe when you accept glory from one another and do not seek the glory that comes from the one who alone is God? (Jn 5:41, 44)

Jesus was single-minded. His life's purpose was to discern the Father's initiatives and pay the price of cooperating with the Father to establish the reign of God.

Appearances, what others may think of us and say about us, and what may bring us benefit in the sight of others, greatly influence what we say and do. What are the influences and 'gods' that guide your life? Be specific in seeking the help and grace you need to live like Jesus, who always sought the approval that comes from his Father.

Day 6

> For by grace you have been saved through faith, and this is not your own doing; it is the gift of God – not the result of works, so that no one may boast. For we are what he has made us, created in Christ Jesus for good works, which God prepared beforehand to be our way of life. (Eph 2:8–10)

God's grace is ever new. This is a privileged moment of his grace for you. It is all God's work. You cannot claim the credit. It is he who has opened your eyes to the mystery of his greatness and calls you to make him known in the marketplace. Hear a prayer of gratitude and praise surface in your life.

Day 7

> Just so, I tell you, there is joy in the presence of
> the angels of God over one sinner who repents.
> (Lk 15:10)

It is easier to think of your own efforts than to think of God's delight and joy in you as you make, with his grace, the smallest gesture towards him. Did you ever think that he took great delight in you as he saw you coming today? You may experience joy when you know his delight in you. Joy is a fruit of the Spirit. It is the natural condition for those who know that God's love enfolds them and that he takes delight in them.

> The greatest honour we can give to Almighty
> God is to live gladly because of the knowledge of
> his love … We are his bliss, because he endlessly
> delights in us; and so with his grace shall we
> delight in him. (Julian of Norwich)

Take some time in silence and wonder before Jesus who delights in you.

Week 6

Day 1

> They devoted themselves to the apostles' teaching and fellowship, to the breaking of bread and the prayers … Day by day, as they spent much time together in the temple, they broke bread at home and ate their food with glad and generous hearts … And day by day the Lord added to their number those who were being saved. (Acts 2:42, 46, 47)

Here we have some central elements of the life of the early Church. People were faithful to and learned from the teaching of the apostles. They gave a focus to the formation of community. They cared for those in need, and they met together for worship and for Eucharist. Their activities, which were aimed at the formation of individuals as people of the community, seemed to be equally based on the temple, and on the home as 'a domestic church'. The result was that many others were being added to their communities. Growth was part of the life of the early Church. Here, now, is a 'checklist' for your path as you come before the Lord. Thank him for the way you live many or all of these elements. Ask for his discernment and grace to live more fully those elements you tend to overlook or to which you give insufficient attention.

Day 2

> For where two or three are gathered in my name,
> I am there among them. (Mt 18:20)

There is a real presence of Christ when you meet with people in his name, whether with your family and friends or in a prayer gathering with acquaintances. Bring before the Lord today your prayer for a deeper Christian fellowship, where you recognise him as you gather with others, and where you will receive support on your journey with him.

Day 3

> But you are a chosen race, a royal priesthood, a
> holy nation, God's own people, in order that you
> may proclaim the mighty acts of him who called
> you out of darkness into his marvellous light.
> Once you were not a people,
> but now you are God's people;
> once you had not received mercy,
> but now you have received mercy. (1 Pet 2:9–10)

You have a song to sing. You have praises to express. God calls you to sing his praises. He calls people as individuals to service of others and to experience community with them. He is calling you to peoplehood, to be part of, and involved with, his people. Now, put your roots down amid the new thing you see he is doing; amid the people he is calling to a living faith. Lift up your heart and voice in praise of God.

Day 4

> Let the word of Christ dwell in you richly; teach
> and admonish one another in all wisdom; and
> with gratitude in your hearts sing psalms, hymns,
> and spiritual songs to God. And whatever you do,
> in word or deed, do everything in the name of
> the Lord Jesus, giving thanks to God the Father
> through him. (Col 3:16–17).

A saint is sometimes described as one whose inner
convictions conform to what she or he says and does. It
is letting the message of Christ find a home in you and
seeking to live it with commitment and authenticity. In
today's scripture passage you find guidelines about sharing
faith with others, and about what you do when you meet.
It is primarily taking time to let the message of Christ sink
in, sharing wisdom with one another, expressing gratitude,
giving thanks and being led by the Lord.
Allow the Lord to dream his thoughts in you today as you
pray.

Day 5

> When they have a dispute, they come to me and
> I decide between one person and another, and I
> make known to them the statutes and instructions
> of God.' Moses' father-in-law said to him, 'What
> you are doing is not good. You will surely wear
> yourself out, both you and these people with you.
> For the task is too heavy for you; you cannot do

it alone. Now listen to me. I will give you counsel, and God be with you! You should represent the people before God, and you should bring their cases before God; teach them the statutes and instructions and make known to them the way they are to go and the things they are to do. You should also look for able men among all the people, men who fear God, are trustworthy, and hate dishonest gain; set such men over them as officers over thousands, hundreds, fifties, and tens. Let them sit as judges for the people at all times; let them bring every important case to you, but decide every minor case themselves. So it will be easier for you, and they will bear the burden with you. If you do this, and God so commands you, then you will be able to endure, and all these people will go to their home in peace.' (Ex 18:16–23)

The experience of many people in ministry is like that of Moses. In extreme cases it is called the 'danger of burnout', due to excessive demands and expectations. At the same time, many people feel that the Church does not care for them. It remains too distant from them. They feel they belong to a great anonymous crowd, an institution, rather than a community. In today's scripture a clear role for spiritual leaders is outlined. They are to be teachers towards wisdom. However, they are not to do everything. Their primary task is to come before God in intercession for those for whom they have responsibility. They are to select and train guides who will care for the people. Their strategy then is to place all the people into small groups or communities, with a trained guide. Instead of shedding all responsibility, the decisions and matters of consequence will be referred back to them. For the one with responsibility, it will mean fewer burdens, with more time for personal reflection and prayer for all the people. At the same time, each person benefits while many people are formed to take on pastoral responsibility. What may the Lord be saying to you about all this as a strategy of renewal? What does it mean for you?

Day 6

> Now you are the body of Christ and individually members of it. And God has appointed in the church first apostles, second prophets, third teachers; then deeds of power, then gifts of healing, forms of assistance, forms of leadership, various kinds of tongues. Are all apostles? Are all prophets? Are all teachers? Do all work miracles? Do all possess gifts of healing? Do all speak in tongues? Do all interpret? (1 Cor 12:27–30)

(It may also be helpful to read verses 4–13.) The witness of any community is much greater than the individual witness of all its members. The body of Christ, and each community, is called together by God. The Spirit of God inspires a multiplicity of gifts so that the community will be well organised, and especially that it will impact the prevailing culture through miracles, inspired teaching, interpreting the events and trends of the day (prophecy), words of faith, healing etc. A community is effective when each person offers his or her own giftedness, whatever that is, as inspired by the Spirit. There is no room for jealousy, only listening to the Spirit of God and encouragement of one another. Entrust your life to the Spirit of God, and seek his guidance in the areas where you are looking for answers. What is the unique touch of the Spirit of God in your life? Where is he calling you to belong and to serve?

Day 7

> After this the Lord appointed seventy[a] others and sent them on ahead of him in pairs to every town and place where he himself intended to go. He said to them, 'The harvest is plentiful, but the laborers are few; therefore ask the Lord of the harvest to send out laborers into his harvest. Go on your way. (Lk 10:1–3)

Do you know that you are being sent to prepare the ground, to break a furrow, so that the Lord can come and reveal his presence? To whom are you being sent? From what community and base are you being sent? With whom will you go?

In your time of prayer today, dream the Lord's dream for you and be attentive to the promptings of his Spirit for your life.

Review the last six weeks and thank God for the opportunity. Has there been a special grace or insight for you? Where is God now leading you on your pilgrim journey?

Section 3

Daily Reflections and Personal Prayer

Chapter 4: My Good News Story

YOU HAVE a faith story. You may, or may not, have reflected upon it to any great extent. You have an experience of life, and a relationship with God, which are different from anyone else's. Your faith story includes moments of grace when you realised that God was with you. These may have evoked a generosity that led you into a deeper trust in him. You may be able to remember a very significant moment, which occasioned a profound conversion in your relationship with God.

You may feel your enthusiasm has waned. You may have known personal and/or family difficulties, which tested your belief in a God who loves you. You may have felt alone in your following of Christ, yet he has not remained silent. You may realise that a particular graced moment continues to exercise a profound impact upon you. As you reflect you may see that your story is not simply one great uninterrupted event of moving forward in faith, but carries grace and sin, enthusiasm and apathy, commitment and failure to commit, hope and despair. And yet you may sense that all the while a deeper trust, perhaps a deeper poverty, is being born in you, and you are being transformed to the person God has desired you to become.

As you reflect, you may recall two ways you see the action

of God in your life. Firstly, the time when you knew that the Christian story was real and true for you and not simply a set of beliefs, rituals and codes that you had accepted on the basis of what others had said. It became a moment of decision when you decided to give a greater place to God in your life. The guidelines given below are drawn up with that moment in mind, when you can more clearly identify it and describe it in writing. They will help you to clarify your story and recall the circumstances and the changes it led to for you.

Secondly, you recall the many times when you knew that God was helping you through difficult situations. The guidelines below can also help you to learn about moments of God's guidance, wisdom and support for you during your life. You may have been aware of them, and/or perhaps had taken them for granted or forgotten. Looking again at these times will serve to deepen your faith and trust in God.

The great value of this exercise is that you will know that you have a story to relate, which no one else can contradict, simply because it is yours. Should you ever wish to tell your story it will leave a profound impact. It is really the story of God active, living and making a difference in your life. It needs to be told in a way that is sensitive to the situation of the hearer, in a language and manner that is genuinely your own, without seeking to impress. It is best related with love and humility in your own words and without using religious jargon to impress the hearer. Essentially, you share your story as an act of gratitude to God who is its real source.

Decide on a day and time when you will complete the exercise below and set out your own story. Write it as a continuation of your prayer time on the day of your choosing. There are three stages in putting together your story. It is important to be specific and give real examples as you complete this exercise.

1. *Describe aspects of the way you lived and the way you saw things before the event.*
   - What was your life like before you came to know Christ in a more personal way?
   - What were some of your attitudes? Your values? Your questions? Your difficulties?
   - What largely took up your time? What engaged your thinking time?
   - Where did you seek security and contentment?

2. *Describe the actual change and what led to it.*
   - What led to your deepening trust in Christ? Why did you decide to take this step at that particular time? What was happening in your life at that time?
   - What were your reactions when faced with this decision?
   - Describe the precise moment of change for you. When and in what circumstances did you come to a deeper trust in Christ?

3. *Describe the way things are for you since that time.*
   - What changes did you see in your life? In your actions? In your attitudes?
   - When did you recognise that changes were taking place in your life? Describe some of these changes.
   - Who is Jesus Christ for you now and what is his influence upon you?

There is often a temptation to over-exaggerate and to see everything as wonderful. It is important to be aware of the real situation of your life with its continuing questions and difficulties, while knowing the providence and action of God.

Write out the answers to the questions above. When completed, what you have written should take about three minutes to read. You now have a 'Good News Story', should you ever wish to stand up and tell it to a group. More importantly, your writing will have brought clarity to your thinking that will be of great help to you in one-to-one conversations.

This exercise is purely for yourself so that you become more sensitive to the action of God's Spirit, who has been, and is always, at work in your life. It is completely at your discretion should you ever wish to share it with another.

I conclude with what I consider a very powerful statement on the gradual unfolding of God's plan in the experiences and events of daily living.

> From eternity God has thought of us and has loved us as unique individuals. He has called every one of us by name … However, only in the unfolding of the history of our lives and its events is the eternal plan of God revealed to each of us … a gradual process … that happens day by day. (Pope John Paul II, *Christifideles Laici*)

Chapter 5: What Happens Next For You?

Obviously, it is over to you. It all depends on what you sense is best for you, or what you think will be of greatest benefit. I suggest one possibility, with which I have close connections, namely, parish cell communities. People tell me they find them helpful, especially during difficult times. They say they find meaning and confidence when they are unsure and uncertain as to what they believe in.

A parish cell community is a group of four to twelve people who meet, normally in homes, to grow in understanding God's love for them and to see how they can best live their faith in daily life. There is no great magic about a cell community. It all depends on whether you see such a group as a good next step for you. If you think yes, or are simply curious, much help is now available (see below). You can easily set one up. You simply begin to speak of your thinking to a few other people. As you do so, you seek their help and trust in God's wisdom to guide you.

A parish cell community is also much more and much richer than the help that individuals receive. People say that a personal relationship with Christ opens up for them, and, as it does, they become more contented, open to seeing God in all things, and more thankful. They also tell of a new facility, which helps them speak with friends and members of their families in a natural and respectful way about the meaning of God.

Moreover, I have seen cell communities exercise a

profound impact within parishes where they exist. As people listen together to the scriptures and respond in prayer, hear teachings on aspects of faith and Christian living and listen to one another tell stories of the influence of God, their faith matures and a genuine service of people and a missionary outreach are born. Such individuals then enrich parish life.

The greatest benefit of parish cell communities, as I see it, is that it offers the experience of Christian community. In 1989, when I first heard of these communities I was on my own personal search. My previous parish experience had taught me that only a minority respond to advertised talks or courses. I was thus searching for ways to involve a wide number of parishioners in conversations of faith.

Then came what I now call one of God's surprises for me. In November 1989, I heard Don PiGi Pe
rini speak about almost 100 parish cells, almost 1,000 people, in his parish at St Eustorgio, Milan. This attracted me.

I loved the idea of small Christian communities in a parish that would reach out to others and grow by multiplication. What I heard continued to haunt me. Then in 1990, I attended the International Cell Seminar in Milan, accompanied by three fellow parishioners. What we experienced influenced us deeply. And within two years, there were thirty-one small communities in the parish of Ballinteer. This meant that more than 300 parishioners met each fortnight in small communities in their homes to share God's word, and commit to sharing it within their relationships of home, neighbourhood, work and leisure. This is one example of a parish cell community in Ireland.

I believe the future of Christian faith in Ireland will depend on local communities, where people are formed in faith to discern, celebrate, announce and live the wisdom of God as Good News. Parish cell communities are one method of growing small faith communities. They have helped me to dream that a parish as a community of communities is possible, with emphasis upon families and little home communities who join together at Sunday Eucharist. They also provide me with a method and system that helps me in pursuing this dream.

I recently received an email from Martin, a layperson who is very involved in his parish. In it he wrote: 'Parish cells are a very powerful way forward for living Christian community in the twenty-first century. Those who are passionate about seeing Church renewal would do well to recognise the gift that they are. Perhaps their time has come.'

In September 2015, Pope Francis met 5,500 worldwide cell participants in Rome. He spoke about the importance of the cell charism of evangelisation. He said, 'You have the vocation of being like a seed through which the parish community examines its missionary existence, and for this reason you feel irresistibly within you the call to meet everyone to proclaim the beauty of the Gospel. Meeting in homes to share the joys and expectations that are present in the heart of each person is a genuine experience of evangelisation which closely resembles what took place in the early times of the Church.'

For further information on the format
of meetings, history, benefits etc.:

ONE:
Website: http://www.parishcellsireland.net/

TWO:
Contact your nearest parish cell community.

May the Spirit of God guide you.